Like the Rains Come

Also by Mercedes Roffé:

In Spanish:
Poemas (Madrid, 1978)
El tapiz de Ferdinand Oziel (Buenos Aires, 1983)
Cámara baja (Buenos Aires, 1987; Santiago de Chile, 1996)
La noche y las palabras (Buenos Aires, 1996; Santiago de Chile, 1998)
Antología poética (Caracas, 2000)
Canto errante (Buenos Aires, 2002)
Memorial de agravios (Córdoba, 2002)
La ópera fantasma (Buenos Aires, 2006)
Milenios caen de su vuelo. Poemas 1977-2003 (Madrid, 2006)

In French:
Rapprochements de la bouche du roi (Montréal, 2008.
                    Translated by Nelly Roffé)
Définitions mayas et autres poèmes (Montréal, 2004.
          Translated by Nelly Roffé, with a Preface by Hélène Dorion)

In Italian:
L'algebra oscura (S. Marco in Lamis, 2004. Translated by Emilio Coco)

In Romanian:
Teoria culorilor (Bucharest, 2006. Translated by D. M. Ion)

In English:
Theory of Colors (chapbook. New York, 2005.
                    Translated by Margaret Carson)
Trial by Ordeal (chapbook. New York, 2002.
                    Translated by Janet Greenberg)

Like the Rains Come

Selected Poems 1987-2006

MERCEDES ROFFÉ

Translated by Janet Greenberg

Shearsman Books
Exeter

First published in the United Kingdom in 2008 by
Shearsman Books Ltd
58 Velwell Road
Exeter EX4 4LD

www.shearsman.com

ISBN   978-1-905700-55-4

Contents

Like the Rains Come

For Donald Howe

from
The Lower Chamber

A scene of return is drawn
Voices
National language   the music
of the spheres
Perhaps because of being in the air
Because of being
               in flight
Because of being
               in transit
Transit
     Synagogue of the
The detailed catalogue of the tribe
     Ceuta
        Tangier
            Oran
The fleeting prison
the bangles
the myth of the Moor and the old songs
The intersection: seven languages
Casablanca:
     the end of a tale that is never told
          but counts
Oran:
     the name that circumcises that which is said to be
         uncircumcisable

Without the A there is no concert
        just Solos
Transit
Scene of return
The angel comes to transfix a lung addicted
        to the literary tradition
The whitewashed tradition of a convent
You confuse a headquarters with a convent
        the same
as your
        daughter's
        mother's
        grandmother's house
Orthopedics
        WANTED
The mirror
Your fate on a piece of paper
A convent, wants
A white enclosure in which
to be
        traversed
        transfixed
        wedded to
Father and master
You, who fears the lyre
        sing to me
                tell me
                        make me
                                endow me
                                        cover me
He who fears the lyre
        the music of the spheres
Won't arrive
Slanting view
Father

Mother
Uncle
Aunt
What am I doing here?
I run away to a party
A party
quickly!
A party
Remember me
It's me
I'm here
There is no party without gods
A fellow called . . .
A fellow called . . .
Mesié Fifí!
Mesié Fifí!
Oh flame of love
The king dies
The king has died
Long live the king

He said:
       "too pointed a discourse"
And the green elf sang in falsetto:
       "Be sharp, darling! Immortalize
     this Ianthean silhouette
         Don't be
       a bad girl,
           eh?"

She said:
       "Be more yourself"
And the green elf choked on the wine

It's been two years
assuming that it . . .
Two years of what?
It was cold
Two years ago it was a title for a poem without name
        and the open sheets among Rilke's shrouds
All the amber
Me
All the amber from afar that came in ships
Like me
Amber like the eyes of the sirens
She isn't a siren
But
All the amber had come in ships for the feast
Oh night sweeter than the dawn
Transfigured night
The waiting
So Parisian!
The beret with a visor and the scarf
A melancholy, little, trembling pimp
A betrayal at the hands of *the-much-awaited-one*
The beloved with the beloved
The beloved transformed in the beloved
So Parisian! It flies away
Her face appears on the walls of an office restroom

like obscene, political graffiti – X loves – Death to the
traitors – Barbarians – and the dead – X loves – 781-1452
– Spitting forbidden – Screaming forbidden – Speaking
forbidden – The two names together forbidden – The
one who squeals is – the one who doesn't
Her face on the wall
of an office restroom
    of a bar
        a school
The little school, yes
The grapevine
It was easy for me then
It was not necessary
It was not necessary to tell you I hate you
I didn't have to say
I didn't have to look, listen, know
that all the sirens' eyes
are the color of amber
I didn't
have to come on that ship and then
perhaps I would have never ever
Transfigured night   x   Night in the Gardens of Spain

Today, like today
like that night
a night
a night all filled with murmurs
all of it
all of it
dance for the big toe of the right foot
trembling dance for the little pimp
It was cold
Shivering underneath an embroidered shirt

Shirts worn by grooms at their weddings
Embroidered shirts
Shirt underneath the bullfighter's vest
Shirt the priest
    the surgeon
Shirt
Shirts worn by pimps at their funerals
and berets with visors
Parisian
It was cold in the open sheets of
Me—the beloved in the beloved
Dawn
The night transfigured in forgetfulness
Never more
Here nothing has happened
It was for thee
For thee it was
which dog will lick what you leave
Agape
Without gods there is no party
Trembling
Poor little one, the scrounger
almost flying
It was the music of wings
It was amber

It's not about being
It's not about being as one is
It's about
      coming out well
It's not necessary to wax
It's not necessary to have
        your cavities filled
It's not necessary to weigh
           to measure
           to be
                older
                younger
A light effect
The shadow
good paper
It doesn't pay to have the eyes of the sirens
It doesn't pay
     to speak
     until you drive the sailors mad
It doesn't pay
to have thrown yourself through the window last night
   —where there was no glass: interrupted faintings
It's about coming out well
like in a shipwreck

Thou shalt not worship false idols
Thou shalt not utter my name in vain
Thou shall adore false idols without uttering
           their name
until your house becomes a maze
In the blessing of Abraham
     your name was written

A dandy
   a young boy
      a Jewish girl
         a dancer from Algiers
      Arnaut Daniel
   Johnny
      Brunilda
         Isabel Freire

              THE LIGHTHOUSE OF ALEXANDRIA

Yes, the time
yes
Two years
There can't be rituals without time
Time to laugh and time to cry
Time to blaspheme and time
   to read the prophets
There wouldn't be rituals otherwise
like today
"Today makes . . ."
"Today would make . . ."
       say the mothers and the brides
           of the dead
Then
      Now
What might have become of you
   my vine
For whom are you now said to be

Time to discover and time to lose
       each other
Time of birds and time
        of crossroads

There won't be rituals otherwise
A season comes and goes
     my candid sun on a cold day
face of sun
face of fields and milk
kalé hemerá for your eyes
kalé hemerá
     for the whisper of the river
Who will cultivate those corals
Who will collect those corals
        from the water beds

The tablets, remember?
"There was another first day"
There was
          the blood of another woman
          then mine
Who will gather them?
Who will remember them?
Who
     will orchestrate the Hallelujah?

My day won't change
My life
            won't change
Until
I pull back my hair
You give me a brief kiss on the brow
            and say: it's over
Then you the last
            may close my eyes
It's all the same
Help me to bury myself
One shouldn't ask
One shouldn't ask the one who's leaving
It's simple:
            one will ask and remain without it
One can't ask
There's nothing to ask for
The little school
Teaching the children
Everything should be sought without words
Everything should be demanded
            in silence
The only dignity
Watch your eyes
                —betrayal
Watch out

Aserrín
Aserrán
She looked like a young boy
Dance for the big toe of the right foot
La mer
I felt bad
Bad?
Half-open mouth
Burgundy
S p r e a d   i t   o u t
There was blood
There was
blood
You weren't going to kill me
We weren't going to die
Dawn
would come
Coffee and milk for the little pimp
That morning he would lose his fortune
Dawn of a cold day the sirens' eyes
like amber
and the pebbles
and the fortune
the conquerors came
in galleys

Sister Ana, sister Ana
tell me what you see
A single shadow
A single shadow
A single long shadow
I'll see her skin in the galleys
her hands

               her voice I'll hear
            her eyes
         letters
       like hair
      like a mouth half open
Burgundy
The foreigner came
                    in galleys
In ships
The foreigner leaves

Sister Ana, sister Ana
            tell me what you see
Men like ants in the woods
     ta ta
        ra ta ta...
A hum
A hum of bees
It doesn't change me
What calls doesn't change me
The leaves pressed between the pages
                    won't change me
          dry
                green
                    yellow
Mmmmmmmosssssssssssssssssss!
Albertine's dream like a silk worm
It's not the same dog that eats me in its mouth grinds
          our bones
STERNUM
My hand is cupped and filled
I fill you
I tire you
I sate you

I bore you
I bore myself too
We've been since long ago coming in ships and saying
The-same-things
    the girl
        love and hate
            I suffer
                we are crucified
The foolish plot:
            a piece of wood
                    set upon
            another piece of wood

The intersection:
        Nobody blinded the Minotaur
A single shadow
We've been calling Nobody for a long time
            a single shadow

I'll thread beads
I'll try pottery
I'll design bridges
I'll build walls
I'll tie sneakers
I'll do the wash in the river
There was
            your face in the galleys

Cancer gnaws me from shoulder blade to spleen
I wait for
            the last puff of a Dutch tobacco
            sweet and redolent of chocolate
Or
    a pipe leaks and I hold
    with one hand the lead
    a blow torch
    with the other, my legs
    in the bathtub, my head . . .

The light, quick
It's indispensable that you come:
            the light
The feigned blindness
            weak

All ploys are in vain if they're not enough
    (It wasn't enough)
But I didn't let you leave
I didn't try hats on in the stores
Nor will I exchange you for a lacquered
                Japanese table
It wasn't me
                I'll
build a fence

A fence with my arms first
   with my legs
   with my mouth
   with silence
  I'll build
a fence
  of wire
  of music
        of
  aromatic sauces
I'll do it
It won't be easy for you
   No
Old ballads I'd hang from one end of a rope
       to the other and clothes
       that only suit you
I won't do it
  I'll build a fence
  I'll make a basket of wicker and satin and pillows
  and foam
With the names you love I'll make it
  and I'll be discreet enough to omit mine
With the stars just as they were on the day you were born
With the moon just as it was the night I was born
There will be one fate
     one lot
A silly opera in which I'll go crazy and you,
  as befits you, flee
A cello will insist
A shred of something that might have once made you cry
  I'll look
and with everything that causes your laugh I will dye the waters
Everything will be flooded
  yes
Everything will be

        your laughter
Everything is
    I'll build it
in such a way
    that it won't be left entirely closed
I won't build it
    no
    entirely closed
    the fence
        no
You'll be able to choose
I'll be able to know
    or not
Chance
    will be at play
You'll make a game of chance for me that will be
                    my story
                    my laughter
                    my music
                  my silence
                    my
            aromatic sauces
            and perhaps
some sweet tobacco in a porcelain pipe bowl
with an indecipherable inscription on one side
I'll do it
You'll do it
The witches at the base of the statue failed to seduce me
You don't have a dog
and no church will ever know of us
Dances will ignore us and no girl
    will pronounce our names
A challenge
    a challenge
Cancer

gnaws me
from shoulder blade to spleen
The hotel room is flooded
THE LIGHT
Perhaps, this is the night I die

Why not
    eh?
Perhaps I have lost control of my sphincter
    and someone will have to change me
                clean me
                dress me
                prepare me
You can't say no
I haven't had a wet nurse
                you shouldn't
Better yet, perhaps:
        my grandmother has died and on
        occasions like this no one should
        be left alone

All ploys are in vain
if they're not enough
If you don't come everything will be
        in vain
I didn't have you
    give up the piano
I didn't have you wait for me to take a drive
I won't change my nose
I won't lose a child
I won't revere the Illustrious One
I'll call the illustrious to the fence
They'll do a round for you

a round
   they'll do
I promised you

Soul, dear little soul
I know you want me
      to say it
that I hate you
Oh yes
   how much
   how much I hate you
How easy it is
     see?
See, my love?
   I can say that I hate you

Cancer gnaws me
    a tobacco
    a name
I haven't
    tried on
    hats in the stores
I haven't let you
   leave
I won't change my nose
I won't gather
   the traces
I will ask no one about you

Bury it
        Bury it
it wasn't buried
Soul
Dear little soul
Something didn't go well
The papers
A dog
Something
        something
Little soul
A poem by Shakespeare to Sir Leonard Douglas Middleton . . .
Dedication for the Day of the Dead
Soul
Dear little soul
how good, eh?
  how good
that one's husband loves them
Oh how good
            Jeremy
                Tommy
                    oh no . . .
how was it?
Oh, yes
        a lake
Go, little soul

go
    quiet the lake
Go, little soul
    go
    the birds, get going, be a good girl
        tell them
    to be quiet, eh?
To the clouds
    to be quiet,
            eh?
He can't hear
            He can't hear
Get going, little soul
        tell them
Bury them
Bury yourself
Bury them
    Oh, don't forget
    the girls
Bury them, too

Darling,
Dear little soul
what are you doing
                up at this time?
with your little girl's shovel
            what are you doing?

Darling
        the girl, don't forget, my love
    my dear wife
                Go
I am your Haemon

your Shakespeare
           your young Douglas
                      I am
WHO I AM
           Go
The birds,
           don't forget
—Sir, the birds...
Don't insist, girl
   and shut up and
go bury it and
   Oh,
I forbid you to bury it

Darling
Bury them
   Not one word more
I can't hear them
        I CAN'T
Bury them
Bury yourself
Take
        your little girl's shovel
        Go

Darling
Little soul
a tea at your side smells like
        the hortensias and the heavy rains
Little soul
        remember
        a cat
is forever
—And a diamond?

My burnished diamond
—And a harbor?

My old lady
        my dear little soul
                my Lili Marlene
Don't sing
For the dead, Lili
For your magnificent
                foolishness
for me
for him
for the anonymous, Lili
don't sing

"She would have liked to have a romance"
"She would have liked to have a romance with him"

Darling
Dear little soul
Bury yourself
Bury me
Don't sing

From
Night and Words

1. Three Preludes

forty seven degrees in Central Park
a cup of coffee in the morning
may the butter look thick on the bread
laughter
better yet, mouth
the learned sermon and the medieval
laughter
the complete impossibility of exploding
and the Virgin's shawl
and the sweet lamenting
and the silly joke
sic et non
a May afternoon under the bridges
Love shouldn't take lodgings . . .
the son of a clever trick and a drinking spree
there should always be at least one extremely lucid
        and at least another drunk enough
and it should be a May—in Latin "April" but it doesn't matter
full of light and flowers
            a point whatsoever of a May full of light and flowers
            that you'll remember punctually at a point whatsoever
            on the extremely sinuous line of your celibacy, your
            sonorous solitude, your little, private labyrinth, however
            elusive . . .
like picking up the thread, how
to pick up the thread

a May like a triumphal arch a rounded arch a pointed arch an
    arcade an architectural nausea under which to have the
    exterminating angel pass again, the fallen angel, the gullible
    angel, the angel that stumbles a hundred times over the
    same rock
Oh harder than marble
more enduring than marble?
like a tic
like a hiccup
like a droning bass
drops there are that drill
streams there are that flow
submerged cities
and sand castles
castles in the air
moats there are that isolate and guard
and towers of homage —like this one
and there are drawbridges
and chains there are

A white town in the mountains
seventy-five inhabitants
No more than four-hundred teeth total and as many warts
purity
the persistence of the pure
even if the purest is the most depraved
alliteration
nonetheless, you keep looking insisting teaching imparting the
  natural inherent link between the breed and the *p*
everything for that whisper
generations and generations of whispering whispers and the
peteká of champagne on the Russian steppes
with which we arrive to oh! what we wished to demonstrate
thou
and everything just to flee from you
I'll evade you, scoundrel
like children say, "villain, I'll kill you," to their younger brothers
lifting a yellow plastic sword with a pink handle
Abandon realism
Hate the unreachable like the cat, strawberries
And above all, remember that in me, any *vosotros* is not but an
  irony, *tú* a remnant, and *vos* the only unaffected voice
monogram: oil and bull's blood and some of the gold spun in
Arabia
to flee from you
and all just for the sake of living

peteká: epitome of happiness
peteká: signifier of jouissance
but you wanted champagne because you were sad
To flee from you
Where have you seen that?
That's not the way to do it, not like that.
There are rituals, you know
there are rites
The rituals are like
how can I put it?
Like the refrain of a zejel
Like an anaphora
they uphold
they uphold,
like an apocope
Spectat et audit
so quietly
the glands prepare for the ritual
ABACABA
there are things that can't change

. . . they shouldn't

We were talking
but after buying coffee and finding a pseudo-rustic rock next to
        the lake one Monday afternoon in the park
I would have preferred silence
I'm not like that I don't want to I'm not like those
    "what you are turns me away from what you say"
    nor "I like you when you're silent"
the violence of silencing other —usually a woman
of turning her into a landscape
                    a mirror
But by day, by day in spring
her face is so much the day
and her eyes like
like the intersection of a light and a sorrow
so their color their peacefulness and
if the sky could be sad
if something so
could be so deeply and peacefully and resignedly sad
Well yes, mea culpa, I'm ashamed
I'd have enjoyed at her side
the coffee now cold, the lake, the day
in silence
but she spoke
she spoke so much, so much
that it made me long for
the day and the others,

the young and the so old who can be silent
and for her
a longing as long as an evening shadow
a longing for her
who was telling such a long story
about a lake, about the fear of suicide
and about mountains
"Faith is a gift," she said
"just like love is a gift," she said
just like contentment

2. Night and Words

Enchantment

As if unfolding
the horn of plenty
ears so fine, slender
precious stones, gold
jade blowpipes
gondolas
crystals like moons
suns like the eyes of a tiger
      barely glimpsed among the leaves
and the rustle of leaves rubbing together
and the ocean
the nocturnal insistence of the crickets
the moon white like a question
or wonder
nights like strings of pearls
sparks like lively streets
and time as wide as a prairie.

Limit

Instead of morning
a wall of mist.
Days fall
         one
         by
         one
like stars.
The light—could have been—
a planet to be invented
a life.
Ubi sunt?
There was
a half-finished
sandcastle.
You preferred the shipwreck.
Not even:
not shrillness or alcohol
        —it's not time for effusion—
Against the glass of silence
the voice cracks
like the moon on the water.

Self Portrait on the Shores of a Frozen River

> *Je ne donne*
> *spectacle que de mon âme*
> L. Aragon

Diamonds
teeth
lime
Carrara
flagstone and granite
A capricious chessboard
without queen or pawn

Sometimes
not even the river flows

High the crest towards the sun
haughty and foolish
scolds and threatens
the warm, clear day
the wave halted like the step
at the hour of Pompeii

Sometimes
not even the river flows

Twitching face, rough
peaks
milky or ashen
        quartz
bits
    of a bursted cupola
salt
rocks
islands
rectilinear
            lotus
brittle fauna
of a candid, lethal tropic
(The compact
blinding
whiteness of the coast
devises
an annoying beach)

Sometimes
not even the river flows

A seagull
breaks its flight, white
Slender, unfolded
        flies over
the calm
    and the flight
adjusts itself to the stillness

Sometimes
not even the river flows

From the blue boulders
the junipers
feign
    a ghastly flower
bronchi
      forever drowned
a calcined and begging
         hand

Sometimes . . .

Incrusted in the inertia
it stabs like a sorrow
the blackness of a branch

Boredom

Tedium
when the day dies down.
Like when a river dies down
and awakens
   the one cradled by the river.

The whisper of the water
that goes
     silent:
Roar—not voice.
Not iris—fog.
And farther behind
    the void.
Moon
  of unmalleable metal
where nothing is mounted
       nor inscribed.
Tedium
    like a kingdom.

Until
   recovering

                    the inhabited
condition of silence.
Like when
      the river dies down
and the one cradled by the river
            finally awakens
or for the first time
            wakes and sees
anchored in the bays of the night
the tartans of dream.

Night and Words

By candlelight
the words
were losing all reality
that bit of weight that drags in their hems
as they hang from the iron S's
the carcasses and their flies.
Fabrication
    —almost a lie.
The obsequious tingling of the tin plate
flatterer of emptiness.
Masquerade
    —almost a lie.
Rings of smoke like souls
take away the breath
of a faint enthusiasm
without voice or past.
Fog
dust
nothing
The *ephemeral*.
How to withstand
      the ignominy?

The inanity of saying
just words
sea   mustache   bingo   caves
   breakfast   rings   book   swords

Nothing is nothing
Close your eyes tight until
the blue
overflows the glass.
"Here, drink.
Let's toast to everything. And give
the credit to silence. Here
you have it."
The inanity of saying
just words
cradle   tribe   grass   ditch   field
                        minstrel   colophon
A hollow
inflated
by the felicitous gymnastics of pronouncing
the echo of a past
      —the final blow of the corvina's tail
against the dry sand.
Guts
Have guts
Let's withstand
         in the illusion of THE LIGHT
the words
will die far away
perhaps in the bend
where desire embraces memory
before the somnambulant gaze of an
                     indifferent or mordant
                                    other

"There's no plot," I said.
"No intrigue or ending."
Only the return. There's no
possible scaffolding. The night
nonetheless
withstands.
Against all gravity, the night
withstands.
It inevitably
        withstands.

from
Trial by Ordeal

I

Even more. Let's think
of mechanical reproduction. Almost a roller coaster. Almost
a waterwheel. An essay of
                    circular poetics. A fall like
a stone, a block,
        an endless story.

III

See how dignified Melancholy looks. As if hyacinths were raining at her feet. As if pushing aside ribbons, tulles, tiny corollas, with the silky tip of her ridiculous pump.

XVII

Metaphor has died.
Nothing resembles anything else.
The smallest fraction of each atom engrossed in the task of
accomplishing its minimum commandment. To endure, every
morning, the effort of being no matter what. The exhausted
anatomy of an elm . . . The contorted stubbornness of pines . . .
The innocuous whiteness of the ice over the lintel.
The urine of the neighbor's dog traces a groove in the snow.
Insignificant. No more
than all of the rest. No more
than this rash will, the unavoidable inanity
    of this attempt.

XVIII

They saw Christ suckling the dogs. They saw a void in the heart's place. They saw a heap of hay, a Dumbo's ear, an ox's tail, a grain of cooking salt, a hangar, a telescope. They saw a battle between angels and demons in the depths of a tank. And then the rains came, the rains. Obstinate. Sharp. Intermittent. Impatience's nails tapping on the glass. The hours' teeth sputtering the rosary of tedium.

XXVII

Tighter and tighter, the horizon. Broader and broader. Diffusion. Difference. As it is said of a transmission—deferred. An assumption of power, an event, a game . . . An hour that is not. Which was and which is now verified, feigned and accepted, like a rite. A therapeutic / repetition. Monuments. Memories. Constructs. History or creation myth. Mise en scène of a past which explains, suggests, founds, gives a raison d'être to a present somehow failed, imperturbable.

XXXI

The scene so feared—finally—
is now taking place. There, always, on the other side. There
is no poetic justice. Who narrates, otherwise? Or was this the
wish? Which audience's expectation? The dreamer who dreams
a nightmare, what does he wish? If the entire Comedy is just
the scaffolding of Beatrice's chariot, if Hadrian's empire is just
the measure of a slave's suicidal solipsism . . . can restlessness
be the yardstick that measures freedom? dream, the measure
of the light shed upon awakening? Finding out that the very
thing which in the plot was the object of suspicion, was but the
device—the most blatant one—placed there precisely in order
to conceal all the rest of the absurdity.

The scene so feared is still taking place. Irremissibly.

To be afraid and to know, to dream and to awake *are not*
punctual actions.

XXXVII

A vague recollection of those Takahashi poems beginning—
each of them—"This morning, Her Majesty the Queen . . ." and
then, with the same impassive tone—almost a fairytale—with
the same honorable, restrained ceremoniousness, they shift to
detail the spectacle of the most inordinate corruption.

It is not the anecdote. It's that oxymoron between form and
content that makes of those poems a necessary, useful, social
fact: the poem as myth—in the sense of synthesis and of
conglomeration of meaning; as shortcut for thinking and
feeling, in all its shrillness, a fragment, the intersection of any
two axes of a given reality which, otherwise, would fade in the
minutiae of its own obscenity.

XXXVIII

Some lack of atmosphere. Like a votive lamp. Whoever relates
this to me would be lying. Just a hint of splendor, perhaps a
dubious, divided cause, a sic et non, a concealable pride, a
passionate—but composed—contradiction. Let it be. Fine.
Unexpected placidity. To put aside the urge [moved by the urge].
Two. A back, a neck, a voice: fragments, supported by a way of
being there, firm, a net properly woven. A wait which presents
itself. With such sly discretion. With

total tact.

XXXIX

Prismatic, divided, dispersed vision. A way of not standing in one's place but surrounding it and surrounding the void that is left. Observation: to keep alive the flame of a pure faith with neither cult nor credo nor relic. To keep oneself alive in the faith—an emptiness.

Asyndeton. Apposition. Grammar as anatomy. Theoretical nakedness.

XL

Statics. A vibration or interference. To repeat. To repeat—fear or courage. What is known unpronounceable—except by the eyes. An insistent murmur, local, distinct, properly defined. An exhausting and exhausted (im)possibility. The drop pierces the stone, and the stone the puddle.

Someone paints a screen with green, blue birds, chrysanthemums.
Someone else—a man, a woman—travels down the road of happiness.

from
Mayan Definitions

Sometimes

It is said
when something is not always possible
a habit or a way not very
frequent
not everyday
—which does not mean never
It is usually said when once in a while something
such as feeling sad or lonely or happy or pretty
happens as if we said every so often
one day it does, two days it doesn't
one day it does, three days it doesn't
but not regularly
not every two
or three days
or every Saturday
or Thursday
or two out of four Fridays
but for instance one Friday it does
and then it doesn't
and then, two or three weeks later
it does and then it doesn't for five or six or fifteen days
and then again, it happens.

It might also be the case
that we come to forget something for a while
or somebody
and then we suddenly see it—we assume—
or have it or remember it or miss it once again
somewhat later
and somewhat later one more time
and again and again a little later

Or it is said with regard
to something that happens
usually in the soul
like a rhythm
or with a certain rhythm
that we usually ignore
that we rather recognize
every time
and when we come to realize that it reappears
that it has already appeared many times and we have
recognized it
then we say that it happens
every certain time
every certain measure
of a time we are unaware of
just like feeling like singing or
falling in love
just like the rains come

sometimes

Then

Earlier, much earlier
in the time I am talking about
when I was a child
when my mother was a child
my grandmother
when the war
when the Great Depression Prohibition
when the Mozarabic rite beats in a double ordeal
the Cathar heresy
when they came to America
when Erik
when the Tetralogy
when La Traviata opens at the Colón only five years after
its debut in Paris
approximately when
Cartier had opened and the country
was just emerging from
tyranny
      (see
that there is no guarantee?)
When everything is just that approximate, wrong
evoked, mistaken

like those quotations by Curtius during the War or Borges
in his retentive blindness or Paz
and so many others in the eagerness
　　　　　of their blind ambition

or when
the Egyptians or when
they built the pyramids
the Aztecs
they used to
when
the Sistine Chapel or the Moscow
subway
they used to
when
Caliph Omar or Caesar's soldiers
destroyed
the Library of Alexandria
or Nero, Rome
or God
the Tower of Babel
or the grass
the horses of Attila
　　　　　(where is it now, Maria,
so strenuous, the arrow, suspended in its way
like breath in the mouth
of Tristam's father? The wait is always painful
isn't it? Even to wait for
the end of a sentence, an argument, is painful
don't you think so?)
when everyone destroyed
what was theirs
and had destroyed or assembled or done or hatched or erected

or when the detective goes and finds the body and
or when her husband goes and sees her and the boy
or when his friend realizes it

Then
when it falls
when night
when it comes
everything that comes
afterwards
everything that usually occurs in
the preterit or not
necessarily after
something
only seemingly conclusive
that instead unfolds

Landscape

(Predominantly) natural composition
with certain aesthetic co(i)nci(d)ence or intent
either harmonious or naïve, romantic or uncanny
vivid or spectral
crowded or succinct
—where the "or" doesn't exclude; it adds
at any rate
pampa with tree
tempest in the ocean
Swiss farm with tractor in the background
crenelated wall and slanted, in a Gothic frame
green and undulating field and hamlet
red rock
coal-blackened soil
iron
tarred highway
dark-green olive grove / charred-brown logs
cow
sunset
—and somehow overprinted
may be too close my face
in the crystal—
clouds, clouds

sluggish herd through the blue prairie
and below
like a piece of cloth sewn by a tailor
—basting thread—
trapezes of plowed soil
dried-up yellow
clay
charcoal
asphalt
even more: granite

and the desert?
and the mountains as black as she-wolves?
and the snowcapped, wuthering heights?
And what about dream? and what about
the day at dawn? and what about the resigned
pace of the day that leaves?

And what about the other ones
the lunar and stellar, the oneiric, the submarine, the hyperreal
Malachite and blue-iced caves
horizon in the fox's eyes sniffing out its pray
Or: vertical cut of the planet's womb

And what about the city? what about
that pointy queen? Edges, blades, shadows, needle tips
and on one side, the river
Or will you take *à la lettre*
what's been said
            "green and wooded
rural or inter-
stellar"?

—where the "or" neither
excludes nor adds; being as it is, probably not more than
the aftertaste
of a gesture of surprise a little bit too
self-conscious

landscape of
the land it holds within
o fleeting nest!

cape	sleeveless garment / point of land
	jutting out into water
cap	head covering / overlying rock layer
	usually hard to penetrate
and	conjunction / function word to indicate
	connection between two or more similar things
ape	
pea	
pen	drum / weapon
dance	
sand	warm granular width
end	point where something ceases to exist /
	boundary / far extreme
den	animals' dwelling
pane	glass, crystal
dean	
lend	
lens	as in focus
space	

—See?
That's a sky
That's a willow

Mayan Definitions took their name and style from a series of texts included by ethnologist Allan Burns in his study *An Epoch of Miracles: Oral Literature of the Yucatec Maya* (UTP, 1983), reprinted by Jerome Rothenberg in his anthologies, *Technicians of the Sacred: A Range of Poetries from Africa, America, Asia, Europe & Oceania* (UCP, 1985) and *Shaking the Pumpkin: Traditional Poetry of the Indian North Americas* (UNMP, 1986). Those texts originated in the exchange between Burns and his informant, Alonso Gonzales Mó, who recorded either orally or in writing the meaning and usage of some Mayan words and expressions as a way to help preserve his culture.

Mercedes Roffé is one of Argentina's leading contemporary poets. Widely published in Latin America and Spain, her poetry has also been published in translation in Italy, Quebec, Romania, Belgium, and the United States. In 1998 she founded Pen Press, Plaquettes de Poesía, a successful tiny press dedicated to the publication of contemporary Spanish-language poets as well as poets of other languages in Spanish translation. She holds a diploma in Modern Languages from the University of Buenos Aires, and a Ph.D. in Spanish and Latin American Literatures from New York University. Among other distinctions, she was awarded a John Simon Guggenheim Fellowship in poetry (2001).

She divides her time between Buenos Aires and New York, and is frequently invited to read from her work at international poetry festivals and academic settings around the world.

Janet Greenberg holds a Ph.D. from the University of California at Berkeley in Comparative Literature. She has taught French, English, Spanish, and critical writing at Berkeley, and served for several years as fellowship program director at the American Council for Learned Societies, in New York City. She has published pioneering works on the autobiographical genre and Argentine women writers from the 1920's to the present. Her co-authored publications in this area include *Women, Culture and Politics in Latin America* (University of California Press, 1990). *Like the Rains Come. Selected Poems (1978-2006)* is her first book-length poetry translation.